NO PLACE FOR COWARDS

BY ANNE BERESFORD

Walking without Moving (Turret Books 1967)
The Lair (Rapp and Whiting 1968)
Footsteps on Snow (Agenda Editions 1972)
The Curving Shore (Agenda Editions 1975)
Songs a Thracian Taught Me (Marion Boyars 1980)
Songs from God's Country (Yoxford Publications 1980)
The Sele of the Morning (Agenda Editions 1988)
Snapshots from an Album 1884-1895 (Katabasis 1992)
Charm with Stones/Zauberspruch mit Steinen
(bilingual text: Shriftenreihe Lyrik im Hölderlin Turm, Tübingen 1993)
Landscape with Figures (Agenda Editions 1994)
Selected and New Poems (Agenda Editions & Bellew Publishing 1997)

Alexandros (translation of Selected Poems by Vera Lungu, Agenda Editions 1975)

NO PLACE FOR COWARDS

Anne Beresford

KATABASIS

First published in 1998 by KATABASIS
10 St Martins Close, London NW1 0HR (0171 485 3830)

Printed and bound by Antony Rowe Ltd,
Chippenham (01249 659705).
The cover illustration is of The Demons
(after a poem by Pushkin)
by Fiodor Shilov (1915-1967),
Vladimir-Suzdal Museum, Mstiora

Typeset in-house mainly in 12 point Garamond Antiqua

Trade Distribution: Central Books
99 Wallis Road
London E9 5LN
(0181 986 4854)

ISBN: 0 904872 29 7

British Library Cataloguing in Publication Data:
A catalogue record for this book is available
from the British Library.

KATABASIS is grateful for the support
of the London Arts Board.

To
Veronica
Thomas
Francis
Leah
Naomi

ACKNOWLEDGMENTS

Some of these poems have appeared in *Agenda* and *Babel* magazines and in *Selected and New Poems* (Agenda Editions & Bellew Publishing 1997).

CONTENTS

February for the Crazy Pilgrim 1
The Crazy Pilgrim in Conversation 2
On the Train 3
Message from a Far Country 4
Cold Summer 5
Undressing in front of Chekov 6
The Uninvited 7
Demon Lover 8
Coming to Terms with Demons 9
Tit for Tat 10
Brief Encounter 11
Parting 12
A Quarrel 13
A Dream of Pride 14
A Tempting Offer 15
Big Deal 16
The Haunting 18
George Eliot's Piano Tuner 20
Elgar 22
Night Life 24
Tea Dance 25
Nellie, my Grandmother 26
What do you do all Day while I'm at School? 28
Cathedral Revisited 29
Instead of Writing to You 30
For Dinah who is Glad God is not in her Garden 31
Dichotomy 32
In Memoriam 33
Death on the NHS 34
Past Love 36
Encounter with Hermes 40
Aphrodite 42
The Serpent to Eve 43
Naomi to Ruth 44
Magdalen Dreams into the Future 45
The Hard Core 46
Jairus's Daughter 47
The Other Lazarus 48

Crossing Over 49
Washed Up 50
Credo 52
Finale 54

February for the Crazy Pilgrim

We danced and sang
our voices soared into the night
Eight danced
twelve danced
all numbers being sacred
We kept tune with grace
celebrating life's perfection

And then I thought
how fear is a great enemy
and I cried: Get thee behind me!
I'll not creep through each day
head bowed, feet tentative
Away with the amulets
sprigs of mistletoe
white heather
there's no place for superstition

In the sky the uncountable stars
lit up the melancholy of our fate
No wonder that we sang until
the whistling sands were stilled

Praise be to the morning sun
falling on the aconites

The Crazy Pilgrim in Conversation

Excuse me, comrade,
I have lived for a specific period
and would be merry more often
if I could be acquainted
with this journey which began on foot

It is remarkable
to conceive a desire for a new life
when the present one is only slightly worn
but I am fearful of losing myself
losing the world would be no loss
but imagine losing oneself
imagine looking in the mirror
and not being there

Let me whisper in your ear
take stock of our surroundings
have you ever thought
that we might be in hell already?
That the talk of paradise, utopia
is a left-over dream
from when we were flesh and blood?

No? Well living one's life, comrade,
is not as easy as crossing a field

Now I must continue the trek,
thanks for your company
and remember the moment our shadows
touch the moon
we'll be laughing

On the Train

No longer at ease
in a city
my eyes and ears
are alert for danger
which leaves the burden
on your shoulders

Now in the solitude
of approaching winter
I think how we die bit by bit
at all our partings
how every numbered hair
on our heads
is recounted lovingly
with its change of colour
How the sparrows fall
are lost but cherished

Ah! the forbidden names
of God
how careful we are
to avoid them

Message from a Far Country

Mainly the news from here
is of hedges hacked to death
the first cuckoo of spring
and a green woodpecker sited near the house

An escape from the horrors
which are reported daily in the media
no worse than what has gone before
but no improvement

So now I remark only on the rain
or lack of it. . .

We seem to drift apart on some vast ocean
dreaming of a safe haven

When we finally land
I think we will not recognise each other

Cold Summer

Demeter is back in her cave
sulking. She is afraid that her daughter
has eaten yet another pomegranate seed.

For the last two years
Hades has dominated,
ignoring the agreement.
Persephone looks much paler
and the joyful spring in her step has gone.
At the moment she is resting

Demeter looks out at the grey skies
and watches the corn lashed by winds.
Rain has made everything greener
and it has been a good year for poppies,
but, she thinks bitterly,
that's one of her son-in-law's favourite flowers.

What's Zeus up to? she wonders.
He's been making the earth quake
and sending fiery darts into forests.
Is it time for the end of the fifth race,
his Iron Men? Will he crush them
and burn them from the face of the earth?

My earth, she cries, where my hands tend
orchids, wheat and wild berries,
earth my brother gave me along with our child.
Our child light, fragile as apple blossom
crowned and married to death.
A promise of hope as a wedding gift.

Undressing in front of Chekov

For Vernon Rose, who gave me the first line

This is the house that Chekov wrote
and in the lamplight
a woman stands in her petticoat
contemplating the man she loves.

Far away from Yalta
or Moscow,
in this dacha built on marshy ground,
where laughter and tears
follow a human pattern
and the souls of beautiful women
gaze from windows waiting for something
which might happen,
he watches the nightly ritual
amused as clothes fall to the floor

Is he aware of the axe
taken to rain forests,
cherry trees almost forgotten
water and air no joking matter?

An observer now across a century
his voice out of silence:
'It seems to me that when I die
I shall still have a share in life.'

The Uninvited

These wild horses
which stampede from time to time
through my house and garden
demand to be fed,
vie with the peacock,
the guinea fowl,
claim attention.

To enclose them
in promises of heather-covered moors
proves useless,
to plead work or declining years
only laughable.

They trample on skeletons
not understanding bones,
they know nothing of reality,
nothing of evil.

Uncanny, sensual
they toss their manes,
enticing what is born of the spirit
to rise up and worship an alien god.

Demon Lover

No face
only a presence.
Darkness covers him
yet his invisible strength
holds no kindness.
I never know when next he'll pinion me.
He lurks by my shadow
laughs at my protest
with a hand stifles my screams.

His love pursues me through the years
posing as a tree covered in blossom
a flower with a trembling heart
or a robin with an eye full of questions.

Then he is upon me
breathing deeply into my ear.

Only last night he sneaked into the bed
grasped me tight
conjuring a village and villagers
who could neither see nor hear me.

Coming to Terms with Demons

Mostly they come by night
when the mind is busy.
They land on the bed
with a thud that could wake the dead.

Naked and furry
claw hands and human face
their weight almost stops all breath
a grimace covers the eyes.

On waking limbs are rigid
life slow to return.

These manifestations are a reminder
that three blind maidens spin their web of fate
beneath the roots of the world.

Switch on the light
with dawn the gargoyle leaves.
Now you can breathe again
your past drowned in waters of forgetfulness
your present here
your future lies in other hands.
There must be no despair.

Tit for Tat

He told me:
'You could knock me down with a feather.'
So I did.
Not a large feather
not an ostrich or a peacock
more the size of an owl's.

What people say
or what they mean
is often questionable.
Taking him at his word
came as a shock to him
so when I turned my cheek
he hit the other one.

Brief Encounter

Anima and Animus
met in the bathroom.
He took no interest in her naked body.
Unconcerned
she washed under her arms
and noted how he cleaned his teeth.
His face was blurred
hers, he hardly glimpsed.
'This makes more sense,'
he said,
'than carrying plates to Lowestoft.'
She asked him if he remembered
living in Balham.
No reply.
The building was too public
too many corridors,
Anima preferred a more intimate setting.
Her romanticism always annoyed him.
Animus made off into the night
knowing
she would wait
ever patient
for his return.

Parting

Morning reveals a dead fly
stuck to the window
and wasps snuggling between curtains
whilst a butterfly flusters
around the stove

We've said goodbye often enough
too often
returned again
smiling
with tales of adventure

And now sun
warms the naked trees
lights up a magpie's wing
lessens the icy touch of wind

Perhaps any disagreements
evaporate with early frost
no one can say
if our last goodbye
was final

A Quarrel

A shadow comes between us,
our wills have clashed
leaving me quite incredulous.
Your quiet anger has completely dashed
my hope of lasting friendship.
Foolishly, I thought our minds
were linked in fellowship
not to be torn by winds
of words – right or wrong.
But now you have an axe to grind
leaving me no heart to search among
your past letters which were kind
full of your gentle humorous
soul, which now seems venomous.

A Dream of Pride

What's to be done
with a king who smells of blood
is said to be holy
yet wants to conquer the world?

Marooned in a castle perched on a mountain
below him a plain criss-crossed with streams
his infantry, cavalry, tanks
his pikes, arrows, guns
whatever weapon in season. . .

From his dreaming spires
snug, smug, this king offers gifts
to the oracle and unimpressed by enigmas
orders more soldiers into the fray

But always when thunder darkens the sky
crashes into his sleep
the gods reveal themselves
to prove that no man while he lives can be happy
no man mightier than they

And his son or his daughter
left behind, bereft of speech
holds a bunch of withered flowers
to place on charred bones

A Tempting Offer

Congratulations Mrs H.
You have just won £50,000
or a free heart transplant, your choice.
What you have to do to claim your prize is
reply quickly by signing the enclosed form.
Our computer randomly picked your name
to take part in this unique prize draw.
Don't miss this opportunity
to take up our exclusive offer of a year's
Health Insurance — for half the usual sum.
Or you can buy an Encyclopaedia
for less than the retail price.
We note that in the past
you have missed your chance
of winning a brand new Rover car
double glazing for all your windows
a holiday for two on the Costa Brava
and more much more.
So this time don't be shy,
remember there's got to be a winner
why not let it be you?
One of these days you're bound to fall
and with a name like yours
luck is never far away.
Keep a look out for the postman
we'll be in touch.

Big Deal

In the far off times
where you can't see the woods
because the trees have been felled
and people stand the wrong way up
it happened one day
that two men,
not to mention the woman,
plotted to buy hell.

Naturally they were denounced
but by settling out of court,
the devil, for a vast sum of public money
was quite agreeable to lease his property.

Not entirely what they bargained for
and the woman was a little squeamish
about signing anything with her own blood,
however she has always appreciated
firmness of purpose.

The media will have you believe
that hell is a pit of fire
with a great many naked imps
ready to prod you in awkward places
with tiny pitchforks. . .

As always that's the sensational part,
you have to read between the lines
or rather between the flames. . .
Be that as it may
so far there's no report of a take-over bid
even though this valuable asset
has widened its boundaries.

The Haunting

What were you doing, Savonarola,
on that dark staircase,
doors closed on every landing?
The look you gave me as you sidled past
would have sent me to the stake.

So many people on the stairs
so many monks and priests
and continuous tramp of feet.

The house, tall and foreign,
a cobbled courtyard, long windows.
Not a monastery more a cheap hotel.
One or two old ladies,
garbed in black, gossiping with chambermaids.

You were there mingling in crowds
of new arrivals
your cadaverous face easily recognised
under your cowl.

What were you doing, Savonarola,
in my dream, bidding me welcome
your voice sepulchral?

No flaming sword
no mention of plague or destruction
only people scurrying hither and thither
through murky technicolour.

And you continued down the stairs
leaving me to the final scene of nightmare.
A rope already round my neck
and a child pleading for my life.

George Eliot's Piano Tuner

Tall, thin and consumptive
a lost genius?
Or plump, balding, with podgy hands,
very respectable,
with a son learning the trade
and a daughter learning the piano?
We have no photograph,
no name,
no family background
and but for the annoyance caused
no other mention.
How inconvenient
for the piano tuner.
He must have been quite ill,
very ill,
to have ruined the elegant wallpaper
and the carpet.
Perhaps he ate too many vol-au-vents
at his previous clients
on an empty stomach.
Or maybe the colours in the drawing room
chosen with painstaking care
offended him.
Or was he drunk?
His ears as dizzy as his head,
and disliking the duet played
by the ladies of the house.
We shall never know the true story.
He was discovered
sent home
(if in a cab who paid?) –
much in disgrace,

probably dying of T.B.
or mortification,
his reputation lost —
while the famous fussed and fumed
and asked Mrs Beeton
for hints on removing vomit
from silk wallpaper.
One might be permitted
to call the whole episode
a complete wash out.

In 1863 George Eliot and G.H. Lewis moved into a new house in St John's Wood. Lewis, in a letter to a friend wrote: '. . . besides the trouble and vexation incident to moving we have had extra annoyances. The piano tuner was sick over our elegant wallpaper, which Owen Jones had decorated, and over the carpet. . .'

Elgar

For Esme Sillito

Unless it was his mother's heart beat
words were his first music.
Then as the sun burnt through the mists of summer
birds taught him harmony.

The wand of youth
conjured magic from early grass in spring,
first snow floating to transform
a dark world to one of dazzling light.
Woods around the house filled with melody.
Even the suburbs became a dream
pavements shining blackly in the rain,
and smells of fruit, vegetables
and new baked bread drifting
from the market place of childhood.
All this apart from musical evenings
surrounded by a loving family,
their speech unhurried, life taken
at a *tempo più lento.*

He belonged to another land
and to those who do remember
it has become nostalgic,
seen through a haze of roses.

The dreams of genius came true
but without Alice he would not have risen
above the Malvern Hills.
Son of a piano tuner, married above him —
she fed him on tender care,

quiet in the home — all things flourished
and he drank with a glad heart
until his voice broke from its earthbound roots.

And still his soul was sad.
When the violin or cello cried out for it
his audience sighed, impatient
waiting for more pomp and circumstance.
When he obliged they made him Knight,
Baron, Master of the King's Music
and his soul grew sadder.

After she died
he walked in late autumn
under the trees in brown afternoons
thought of the soft skin on her neck
where her necklace lay.
Those words never spoken.

A last adagio orchestrated in his brain
not meant for human ears,
celebrated by trees
the copper of beech
knotty trunks of oak
vibrating in wild winds
blown from nowhere.

Night Life

In the hotel
guests wander aimlessly
enter rooms without knocking
some faces are familiar
but remain nameless –
not one of them casts a shadow

When morning comes no sun rises
the electricity fails

The word 'escape' on many lips
but how do you escape
from open doors, polite bell-boys
friendly chamber maids?
All paid for by an unknown donor?

Ash trays need emptying
everywhere chaos
little to recommend this place
a labyrinth of corridors

An old French lady tells me
she has enjoyed her visit
she offers me a box of half eaten chocolates
then she adjusts her hat
and seems to evaporate
between two beds and a table

Tea Dance

There is a nostalgia in my soul
for a world without atomic bombs
for things which are small, polite
and harmless.
Please take my arm
together we will fight
the growing tedium of responsibilities
the creeping danger to the bones and face —
an afternoon's escape from those we love
to dance and dance again
touching
light as you will
with eyes averted.

Nellie, My Grandmother

Nellie would have scorned Woman's Lib
She had been liberated for years,
had earned her living from an early age.
No prude, she was down to earth,
gave sound advice.
'Never let your husband know that
you can even boil an egg.'
And: 'Heaven help the woman who marries a virgin.'

Secretly she may have despised men
her father a wastrel and bully,
her husband weak.
When great-grandfather died
she took the family in hand.
Her house in Rowfant Road became its centre.
Packed to overflowing with sisters, brothers,
aunts, uncles and cousins
music seeped through the walls
out into the street.

Children played among grimy flowers,
children practised on an upright piano.
Nellie played her trombone in the bedroom,
Ernest his violin in the kitchen.
Ernest went down in the musical world
while cousins went up, one with her flute
to impress Ethel Smythe,
one, later, with his trumpet
to a prestigious orchestra.

Those in between worked where required,
overtures and interval music in theatres —

ah, those were the days! —
Lyons Corner House or Zeeta's tea rooms.
And some in a band on Clapham Common.
It was pleasant to take tea or lunch
whilst a trio played snippets from Schubert.
Or to stroll across the common
on a fine Sunday evening
and hear a selection from La Traviata,
scent from the Rose Garden wafted in the air.

What do you do all Day while I'm at School?

For Leah, my grand-daughter

Did you expect me to list
the potatoes in need of peeling,
what fish I choose for lunch
or how many times I dust the rooms?

No, no, awake or asleep
I dream, my love,
as most of us do.
Dream of golden horses in fields of cowslips,
peace in a land always beautiful
no wars, violence or hurt.

Like you, I withdraw from the world of reality
my hands grope for the path at night
my feet tread carefully to avoid lines.
Spaces fill with crotchets, quavers
a melody to rise
over dizzy mountain slopes
where prayer-wheels whirl and clatter
and rhododendrons riot.

Cathedral Revisited

For Richard

We have come to bury our dreams
in this cathedral of solemn music
our open coffin, carried by toy horses
halts before the priests robed in gold and crimson
Clowns tumble down the aisle
their cartwheels faster than life itself
and cover our dreaming bodies with a mass of flowers
Perfume fills our lungs
daylight bursts through the roof

We walk out towards another church
built of different brick
where more priests wait –
oh, how patiently they stand
gazing into debris from a thousand bombs

I wrap you with my last strength
and the last remnant of my pride
to protect you from evil
We walk through autumn
already a breath of winter
Wisdom is beyond me

We must find the magic place
where clouds can be brushed away
with sleight of hand

Instead of Writing to You

For Hans Raimund

The wind is mournful
tired of worrying the sea into a frenzy
Instead of writing to you
I am thinking of the fishermen
who told me they get cold six miles off shore
they couldn't swim
The one who spoke had brown eyes
not blue
I tried to find the sea in him
He sold me sprats
dead cod in fish baskets
shivered my heart

You made me aware
of the maypole ribbons
danced by the wind
December sun casting blueness
on puddles deep in the farmyard

And the music of your marriage
played in our house
one summer
sings out from the frozen roses

For Dinah who is glad God is not in her Garden

The sun broke through the clouds
and now late afternoon warmth enfolds this garden
A symphony of bees, flies, birds
join the rustle of leaves
and I think of you lying in the orchard, drowsing

Fantasy on my part
because you are in London
possibly having tea in your own garden
glad of a respite from work
and sheltered from noisy traffic
'No heavenly callers please'
written firmly on your gate

And yet —
we search for the same thing
utopia, God
what's in a name?
We praise buttercups, foxgloves
recognise the Word
our prayers, too, mingle between fields of poppies
and buddleia growing from cracked walls

Dichotomy

For Eva Hoffmann

Perhaps it is the darkness
the division of the soul
or the confusion of aloneness
in a place teeming with life

Some say it is weakness
to see two sides of everything
but still I take the middle way

In your face — tranquillity
in your presence
ordinary day to day activities
become illuminated

Shopping with you in a supermarket
supper on the balcony, candles lit
to keep away mosquitoes,
moments which have become important in my mind
struggling to reach an understanding

To be a participant
in a world of human horror
and a perfection beyond words
is almost a miracle

In Memoriam

Father Lucian Gafton 1996

The sparrow has found its nest
the swallow, flown from the vale of tears

rises
leading the way to a misty world
where silence stands on the point of a needle

Leave behind your memories
joy or sorrow
few of us are saints

Ask nothing
replies come without questions
in a smile or a wisp of smoke from a cigarette

I will see your shadow on the summer grass
hear your voice as a cloud passes
and my body too
will tremble under the sycamore tree
and its heart lie quiet
in the faintest of sighs

Death on the NHS

Tests were carried out
pills prescribed
old people patched up
along with their old cars.

What amounts to an overdose is an overdose
even when unintentional
what amounts to carelessness
is a lack of caring
which leads to feet turning blue under the blankets.

The end was a shattered lamp
paramedics trampling broken glass
and kindness underfoot.

You can't see the dead without an appointment
and with one you must wait
but not here
half in, half out of a busy ward
with telephones ringing
nurses scurrying and raised voices.

Grieving relatives are in the way
especially those who ask questions
especially when doctors
are wanting a post mortem.

We had a last glimpse of her
laid out by a red curtain
hands folded, respectable
not so very peaceful.

Here's a paper hankie
you can't have a glass of water
the carafe is empty.

Past Love

1

Sometimes I still think of you.
It began one afternoon
after your concert.
Vienna wasn't it?
Vienna in the snow.

In a cafe where I sat with friends
eating Sachertorte
you came and handed me a bunch of roses
clicked your heels
spoke tenderly in German
knowing I wouldn't understand.

Our friends teased you
laughed at my blushes
and outside, the snow
thickening on grey pavements
commenced the caprice in a minor key.

2

There is a less romantic scene.
Waiting for you to arrive,
your first visit to my home,
I saw from the window
my great aunt teetering down the street
her black hat awry
her black skirt trailing in the dirt.
And cruelly, in tears,
I begged my mother to intercept her

take her off, somewhere, anywhere but here
where my lover might be shocked
by a drunk old woman
on an unexpected day return to London
lonely for her relatives.

3

You took me to the opera one July
and afterwards we walked across Hyde Park —
summer night in London, warm and smelly.
Under a lime tree you stooped to kiss me.
Suddenly police whistles blew.
'They're clearing the park,' you said.
We ran and as we did courting couples
appeared as if from nowhere
all of us running madly
stumbling from bushes, under trees.
At the gates by Rotten Row,
breathless with laughter,
we wondered why for those five minutes
we'd felt like criminals.

4

Rather than words
a hazy picture hangs on the wall
of my mind — the Green Room
at Wigmore Hall — I came
with the crowd of well-wishers
to murmur or rave about your fine performance.
You were surrounded by people I did not know
culture vultures, critics.
Elated, you flashed your smile

at all and sundry.
Our love, I thought, will be over
as quickly as a scherzo played at speed.

5

In bed you were delicate
your phrasing as perfect as your timing.
Melody flowed through your fingertips
to bruise my heart for ever.
You never raped me
(another man did that at a later date).

6

Days would pass
without my hearing from you.
Angered and sad
I excused you, ready to pretend I understood
but once I saw you in a busy street
with someone else. Dark and chic
she gazed at you with adoring eyes
and you were too absorbed
to notice me slip by.

7

In the end I freed myself
cut the threads
refused to see you.
Oddly enough it was you who wept,
a spoiled boy
wanting something you couldn't have.
And so we parted.

Undramatic, unmusical,
no swan song
only a brief phone call
and then — silence.
But still I think of you
from time to time
in London
or Vienna
your long hands on the violin.

Encounter with Hermes

Long ago
alone in the mountain by Delphi
on his winged feet he flew to me
I leant back into the scent
of wild garlic and narcissus
His voice
deep, loving, caressed my ear
fluttered my hair

High in the blue
an eagle perched on a craggy ledge
his eyes bright

Who would believe
how the earth revolved
in my hot blood
and arms of liquid gold
embraced my nakedness?

Who would believe
in a dream sent from Olympus
to a tourist misplaced by fate?

We bathed in a stream
its banks overgrown with flowers
unfamiliar blue and white

He flew away to the world
of Shining Ones
paused by the temple of Apollo
to listen to music played
on strings of sun

And I took a path
back to the valley
a winding path of stone and moss
stopping to pick up fragments
of broken idols
as the air cooled and Artemis
lifted her bow

Aphrodite

With a look
I can transform
a sensible mortal
to a gibbering idiot

At my altar
heroes fall
swooning
in the fragrance of my incense

Alexandros
poor wretch
worshipped a woman
whose face resembled mine

Beware
of my beautiful gentleness
it can be deadly
with Eros' help
I shatter more than Troy

The Serpent to Eve

My scales are fantastical
so glad you admire them
and how clever of you not to touch me
with hot, sticky hands.

I confess you are as handsome as I am,
from the first moment of your creation
I loved your smooth skin,
and I have loved your curiosity
your self-reliance.

That companion of yours
he is a different matter.
No proper energy, so dull,
he hasn't dared examine this tree
where I coil myself to catch the sun.

Let me tell you a secret.
It's not the fruit
but what the fruit provides
is why you're forbidden to eat it!
Ah, your eyes widen!

Imagine, dear Eve,
what power is like
imagine having powers to match
you know Who!

Naomi to Ruth

We look into each other's eyes
I see your soul
you, mine.
Our own are as alien as the fields
where we have wept
with the loneliness which love
inevitably brings
and with the homesickness of old age.

We are bonded
by the same image
divided into flesh and bone
reflected in the many mirrors on your skirt.

Perhaps words should be
as colours on a canvas
joys and sorrows depicted there
for sharing.

Wife, daughter, mother sister,
our names
threaded from light year to light year —
we are wiser than the next generation.

Magdalen Dreams into the Future

Nuns with long hands
float across the room
their veils touch the ceiling
Once I knew their names

In their charge are silent children
who sit staring upwards, bemused
The stone walls are damp
but the door stands open
sunlight shines in
a diagonal pattern on the floor
and outside wooded hills
call a welcome

When you lay weeping
your unbound hair across my lap
— a reminder of my past —
I watched the nuns finally vanish
back into dreams
and we huddled with those children
fearful of passions
that shake us into the dust

The Hard Core

Why send me here?
This is the convent of the Golden Heart
where it's obligatory to possess a heart of gold.
My feet stick in the generosity and kindness
which flows from the inmates onto the floorboards.
The sweet forgiving voices sicken me
they speak of casting out devils
and healing the sick.
And their prayers, ah God! their prayers
imprison me in ropes of silk.
I scrub and cook in penance for my many sins
guilty of not choosing the better part.
I am eaten alive by sanctity.

But in a moment of recollection
it occurs to me that gold is hard
can lead to misery and crime
is used for crowning teeth which bite.

If my heart was ever gold
it must have melted in the furnace
they call hell.

Jairus's Daughter

People ask:
What was it like?
Was it light
or dark
did you hear voices?

Father says:
Go on, tell them.
His side locks have turned white.

And I thought of the sun
hot as hell
on the beach where the boat landed
and the wailing women
were vultures smelling carrion.

Later I met Lazarus
our pain mingled
in an olive grove
we had no need to speak.

Birth and death
hold no meaning
for those who chase after the wind.

The Other Lazarus

There is a great gulf between us
from the moment of our birth . . .
my sin was poverty
yours thoughtlessness.
Wrapped in a sleeping bag
I lay on your doorstep, burning with fever,
too ill to drag myself away,
too ill even for speech.
I couldn't beg and no one asked me
if I would like some water.
Sometimes a stray dog ambled up
whined in sympathy and licked my face.

In the arms of Abraham
I see your soul far off
burning in the agony of remorse. . .
Lucky, unlucky, life was a game of chance
with obstacles bound to come. . .
and now my peace is shattered
by your voice crying my name.

Crossing Over

It is not forbidden
to go from dark to light
or light to dark
but not encouraged
until the right time

Those who do visit
say little of what they saw
some mention the light
or the dark
some mention a welcome
some murmur of stepping into a smile

On return
the sun shines differently
a quietness falls
even fear evaporates
when the sea rages

No maps are needed
no trekking over mountains
or efforts to scale Mont Blanc
bridges are fictional
so are rivers

Strange how everything melts away
on the border

Washed Up

Sun shines on the sand
the sea blue-grey
and trees rejoice
birds hardly cease their love song

But caught in shallow water
he flounders
panting with an effort to survive

How had it come to this
how could he have imagined
when manoeuvring seas
heavy or placid —
his natural habitat —
that he would land up here

Somewhere in the deep
companions send messages of music
profound music
which Seraphim and Cherubim
understand so well

On the edge of immensity
he begins to fathom
the rhythm of waves
and voices of planets

Too late for regrets
or change
all this time he has dreamt of living
and all this time
he has been busy dying

His body becomes unfamiliar
dry, colder, he can feel it wither
his eyes
dimmed
survey a lost world
and he swallows its beauty
as he would a shoal of fish

Credo

For Paul Hoffmann

As the morning star began to fade
a woman raised her arms
to proclaim the wonder of creation

All things in the heavens
under the sea
and on earth
are confounding, I agree, Lord,
down to the finest detail
no wastage
and to dust we shall certainly return.
Your plan for us is an enigma
we are left with doubts

I have not denied your existence
only marvelled at the evil and the good
which you control
marvel that you took part in the suffering
imposed on us.
Strange and dreadful are the powers of Mammon
is that your other face?
Nothing contains nothing but you contain all.
The seagulls laugh when I ask for understanding
the starlings chatter among themselves
amazed at my ignorance.

Into the darkness shed some light
for the path you indicate
is hardly wide enough for a soul to pass.

In your extraordinary nothingness
take my love with its many facets
imperfect and at times ridiculous —
the tenuous link which holds me to you —
let it grow with the bursting of spring
with the heart of summer
the grief of autumn
the final ice of winter
then say again:
She has loved much.

Finale

These hills are no place for cowards.
Look down — there lies the river
we must cross, no bridge provided
impossible to swim.
Strangely dark and menacing the water
as it gushes over slimy boulders
which are the stepping stones.
The trials so far endured
you've half forgotten.
But now do you notice how ominous the silence?
The emptiness? Not a bird, nor butterfly. Not one.
What lies ahead is Trial by Desolation.
How you cringe! Take cheer,
my timid soul, we've come this far,
no turning back, as you well know.
Pause here for a moment where sunlight
warms our backs and remember
how we floated across meadows
overgrown with daffodils, cowslips
all your favourite flowers
jumbled together out of season.
Remember how flying suddenly became easy
and there we were above ourselves, weightless,
light as dandelion seeds blown on a summer's day.
It grows dark.
No audience left, the curtain falls
before we're done.
We must descend, we've rested long enough.
Gather your courage
soon you'll be alone, without my company
but till we part you'll cling
to my last scrap of flesh.